APPOINTMENTS WITH GOD

150 DAILY ENCOUNTERS WITH THE WORD

© 2005 Michael Kast
Published by Standard Publishing, Cincinnati, Ohio
A division of Standex International Corporation
EMPOWERED® Youth Products is a trademark of Standard Publishing

Cover and interior design by Rule 29
Edited by Dale Reeves

ISBN 0-7847-1541-6

12   11   10   09   08   07   06   05   7   6   5   4   3   2   1

MY WORLD

GETTING TO KNOW MYSELF
AND THE PEOPLE I LOVE

Michael Kast

Standard
PUBLISHING
Bringing The Word to Life™

Cincinnati, Ohio

*To Morgan, my youngest daughter, No. 1
helper and my favorite singer,*

*I love to come into your room each morning to wake you
up, and you look up at me and give me a big hug. It teaches
me a lot about how much God must love us when we talk to him.*

*It's my prayer that, as you get older, you will learn to spend time
with your heavenly Father each day. Your mom and I love to
hear you when you pray and give thanks for everything
you can think of. I'm so glad that I get to be your dad.
I love you with all my heart!*

*Love,
Dad xxooxxoo*

contents

introduction

Congratulations! Just by picking up this book, you are taking the first step toward building a closer relationship with God. That might sound a little scary, but it isn't. The truth is that God loves you so much that he has done some incredible things to prove it to you! As you embark on this journey, you will learn about God, his Son Jesus and his plan for your life.

HOW IT WORKS

To start with, you'll need a Bible, a pen and this journal. Inside you will find 15 different sections, each with 10 Scriptures for you to read. On the first day, select one of the sections, read the introduction and look up the first Scripture. Once you have read it, turn to the first page of the journal section and respond to the prompts:

❖ The main thing I remember or learned from this Scripture is . . .
❖ Here is what God is trying to teach me through this Scripture . . .
❖ As a result of this, today I will . . .
❖ Right now I need to pray about . . .

Then, on days two through 10, you'll look up the next nine Scriptures, one Scripture for each day, and follow the prompts for each day. On the eleventh day you use this journal, select a new section, then read the Scriptures at the bottom for the next 10 days, and so on, until you meet with God for 150 days. Pretty simple strategy, but you'll notice a huge difference in your life as you encounter God and his Word every day.

Take an honest look at yourself and your world. What you really believe, how you spend your time and money. Your friends, those you love, those you need to forgive. When you meet with God, you'll get his take on the things in your life that matter most.

Making It Great

This journal is volume 2 in the *Appointments with God* series. It is important that you keep your appointment with him. Choose a time and place that work for you and give you the space you need to make your time with God great. You've got a divine appointment. He's waiting.

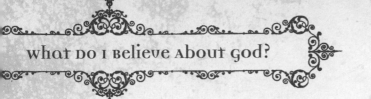

what do i believe about god?

In college one of my projects for a ministry class involved a hands-on experience at a church. A group of us students drove to a small town, where the minister of the church gave us the assignment of going door-to-door, surveying everyone in town. We were to talk to as many people as possible and ask them two questions. First, "If you died today would you go to Heaven?" The second question was "Why would God let you into Heaven?" We divided up the community into sections, were given maps, paired up and started out.

❧ At first I was a little nervous. Most people don't want solicitors coming up to their door, asking questions about dying and going to Heaven. Actually, it was very interesting as we kept notes on people's answers to the two questions. One man said that he would definitely go to Heaven because he himself was a god and would make his own Heaven! A lady said that she would never die. Some people didn't believe that there was a literal Heaven and Hell. They thought that you just died—and that was it.

❧ The majority of people, though, had more predictable answers. Almost everyone felt that when they died, they would go to Heaven—no matter how they had lived here on earth. When we asked them why God would let them into Heaven, we got one of two responses: "Because God is a God of love—he doesn't want anyone to go to Hell" and "Because I've lived a good life and done more good things than bad things."

❧ Wouldn't it be great if we could live however we wanted and then automatically go to Heaven simply because of God's love? Wouldn't it be great if we could earn our way into Heaven by doing a lot of good deeds? Actually, neither of these would be great. While God is a loving God, he is also a just God. And we can't do anything to earn our way to Heaven. God ✓ has already done that for us.

❧ If you ever wonder about God or how to get to Heaven, you'll enjoy learning more during these 10 appointments with him.

appointments with god

Today's Scripture: 1 John 4:9-20
_____

The main thing I remember or learned from this Scripture is . . .
_____
_____
_____
_____
_____
_____

Here is what God is trying to teach me through this Scripture . . .
_____
_____
_____
_____
_____
_____
_____

As a result of this, today I will . . .
_____
_____
_____
_____
_____
_____

Right now I need to pray about . . .
_____
_____
_____
_____
_____
_____

Today's Scripture: Acts 17:24-28 _____

The main thing I remember or learned from this Scripture is . . .

_____

_____

_____

_____

_____

Here is what God is trying to teach me through this Scripture . . .

_____

_____

_____

_____

_____

_____

As a result of this, today I will . . .

_____

_____

_____

_____

_____

Right now I need to pray about . . .

_____

_____

_____

_____

_____

appointments with god

Today's Scripture: John 3:16-18
_____

The main thing I remember or learned from this Scripture is . . .
_____
_____
_____
_____
_____

Here is what God is trying to teach me through this Scripture . . .
_____
_____
_____
_____
_____
_____
_____

As a result of this, today I will . . .
_____
_____
_____
_____
_____
_____

Right now I need to pray about . . .
_____
_____
_____
_____
_____

Today's Scripture: Luke 23:1-46
_____

The main thing I remember or learned from this Scripture is . . .
_____
_____
_____
_____
_____

Here is what God is trying to teach me through this Scripture . . .
_____
_____
_____
_____
_____
_____

As a result of this, today I will . . .
_____
_____
_____
_____
_____
_____

Right now I need to pray about . . .
_____
_____
_____
_____
_____
_____

appointments with god

Today's Scripture: 2 Timothy 3:14-17

The main thing I remember or learned from this Scripture is . . .

_____

_____

_____

_____

_____

Here is what God is trying to teach me through this Scripture . . .

_____

_____

_____

_____

_____

_____

As a result of this, today I will . . .

_____

_____

_____

_____

_____

Right now I need to pray about . . .

_____

_____

_____

_____

_____

Today's Scripture: Romans 3:21-26

The main thing I remember or learned from this Scripture is . . .

_____

_____

_____

_____

Here is what God is trying to teach me through this Scripture . . .

_____

_____

_____

_____

_____

As a result of this, today I will . . .

_____

_____

_____

_____

Right now I need to pray about . . .

_____

_____

_____

_____

_____

appointments with god

Today's Scripture: 1 Timothy 2:1-7

The main thing I remember or learned from this Scripture is . . .

_____
_____
_____
_____
_____
_____

Here is what God is trying to teach me through this Scripture . . .

_____
_____
_____
_____
_____
_____
_____

As a result of this, today I will . . .

_____
_____
_____
_____
_____
_____

Right now I need to pray about . . .

_____
_____
_____
_____
_____
_____

Today's Scripture: Acts 2:36-39

The main thing I remember or learned from this Scripture is . . .

_____

_____

_____

_____

_____

_____

Here is what God is trying to teach me through this Scripture . . .

_____

_____

_____

_____

_____

As a result of this, today I will . . .

_____

_____

_____

_____

_____

Right now I need to pray about . . .

_____

_____

_____

_____

_____

_____

appointments with god

Today's Scripture: Ephesians 4:1-16
_____

The main thing I remember or learned from this Scripture is . . .
_____
_____
_____
_____
_____
_____

Here is what God is trying to teach me through this Scripture . . .
_____
_____
_____
_____
_____
_____
_____

As a result of this, today I will . . .
_____
_____
_____
_____
_____
_____
_____

Right now I need to pray about . . .
_____
_____
_____
_____
_____
_____

Today's Scripture: 1 Thessalonians 4:13-18

The main thing I remember or learned from this Scripture is . . .

_____
_____
_____
_____
_____
_____

Here is what God is trying to teach me through this Scripture . . .

_____
_____
_____
_____
_____
_____

As a result of this, today I will . . .

_____
_____
_____
_____
_____
_____

Right now I need to pray about . . .

_____
_____
_____
_____
_____
_____

appointments with god

what does salvation mean?

I have two friends who both are Christians. They both love God. They both are trying to learn as much about the Bible as they can. They both became Christians in the last year. But these two guys couldn't be more different.

✦ Kurt has a very melancholy personality. He's a perfectionist, very analytical, scheduled and detail oriented. I've jokingly said that he loves to be impulsive—it just has to happen when he's noted on his palm pilot to be spontaneous! Kurt is never late for a meeting. He never messes up his checking account. He plays by the rules.

✦ Kurt's view of God is that God keeps track of everything we do, just waiting for us to mess up. Then God will condemn us to Hell. Kurt lives his life by a list of rules. He's very legalistic in his attitude toward other people. For example, if someone messes up and does something wrong, he questions if that person really loves God and if he is saved and going to Heaven.

✦ My other friend John is the exact opposite. He is very outgoing. He's never met a stranger. He might be standing in line at a fast-food restaurant, and within two minutes he's told a stranger everything about his entire life. He never plans out anything and his favorite two words are *road trip!*

✦ John's view of God is totally opposite from Kurt's. John believes that God's grace covers all our sins. I can't tell you how many times he's told me something wrong that he has done, but it doesn't seem to bother him. He just says, "That's what God's forgiveness is for!" He believes that Christians are free in Christ, and he takes that to the limit.

✦ I fall somewhere in the middle of these two guys. I don't want to live in fear that God is waiting for me to mess up. But I also don't feel comfortable intentionally doing wrong things, assuming that God will forgive my sin.

✦ So which is it? What is this salvation thing all about? For the next set of encounters, you'll have the opportunity to check out what the Bible says about our salvation.

Today's Scripture: Deuteronomy 6:6-9

The main thing I remember or learned from this Scripture is . . .

_____

_____

_____

_____

_____

Here is what God is trying to teach me through this Scripture . . .

_____

_____

_____

_____

_____

As a result of this, today I will . . .

_____

_____

_____

_____

_____

Right now I need to pray about . . .

_____

_____

_____

_____

_____

_____

appointments with god

Today's Scripture: Acts 4:10-12

The main thing I remember or learned from this Scripture is . . .

_____

_____

_____

_____

Here is what God is trying to teach me through this Scripture . . .

_____

_____

_____

_____

_____

As a result of this, today I will . . .

_____

_____

_____

_____

Right now I need to pray about . . .

_____

_____

_____

_____

Today's Scripture: John 10:27-30

The main thing I remember or learned from this Scripture is . . .

Here is what God is trying to teach me through this Scripture . . .

As a result of this, today I will . . .

Right now I need to pray about . . .

appointments with god

Today's Scripture: Romans 3:23; 6:20-23

The main thing I remember or learned from this Scripture is . . .

_____

_____

_____

_____

_____

Here is what God is trying to teach me through this Scripture . . .

_____

_____

_____

_____

_____

As a result of this, today I will . . .

_____

_____

_____

_____

_____

Right now I need to pray about . . .

_____

_____

_____

_____

_____

Today's Scripture: Romans 5:6-8 _____

The main thing I remember or learned from this Scripture is . . .

_____

_____

_____

_____

_____

Here is what God is trying to teach me through this Scripture . . .

_____

_____

_____

_____

_____

As a result of this, today I will . . .

_____

_____

_____

_____

_____

Right now I need to pray about . . .

_____

_____

_____

_____

_____

_____

appointments with god

Today's Scripture: Romans 8:35-39

The main thing I remember or learned from this Scripture is . . .

_____

_____

_____

_____

_____

Here is what God is trying to teach me through this Scripture . . .

_____

_____

_____

_____

_____

As a result of this, today I will . . .

_____

_____

_____

_____

_____

Right now I need to pray about . . .

_____

_____

_____

_____

_____

Today's Scripture: Romans 10:9-13

The main thing I remember or learned from this Scripture is . . .

_____

_____

_____

_____

_____

Here is what God is trying to teach me through this Scripture . . .

_____

_____

_____

_____

_____

As a result of this, today I will . . .

_____

_____

_____

_____

_____

Right now I need to pray about . . .

_____

_____

_____

_____

_____

appointments with god

Today's Scripture: Philippians 3:4-11

The main thing I remember or learned from this Scripture is . . .

_____

_____

_____

_____

_____

_____

Here is what God is trying to teach me through this Scripture . . .

_____

_____

_____

_____

_____

_____

_____

As a result of this, today I will . . .

_____

_____

_____

_____

_____

_____

Right now I need to pray about . . .

_____

_____

_____

_____

_____

_____

Today's Scripture: 1 John 1:5-10 _____

The main thing I remember or learned from this Scripture is . . .

_____

_____

_____

_____

_____

Here is what God is trying to teach me through this Scripture . . .

_____

_____

_____

_____

_____

As a result of this, today I will . . .

_____

_____

_____

_____

_____

Right now I need to pray about . . .

_____

_____

_____

_____

_____

_____

appointments with god

Today's Scripture: 1 John 5:13-15

The main thing I remember or learned from this Scripture is . . .

Here is what God is trying to teach me through this Scripture . . .

As a result of this, today I will . . .

Right now I need to pray about . . .

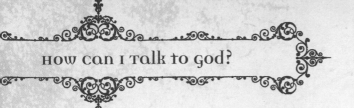

How can I talk to God?

I was flying to Denver, seated in the first row of coach class—the cheap seats. Before takeoff I couldn't help noticing the people in front of me in first class. Their seats were leather and much bigger than my seat. As they boarded the plane, a flight attendant asked if they would like something to drink. No one asked me anything. They got to choose from a variety of snacks. I got nothing! Even though I was seated just one row behind first class, I felt a million miles away.

❧ After takeoff, a flight attendant pulled a curtain so that I couldn't peer into first class anymore. What were they doing? What were they getting that I wasn't getting? I felt left out and a bit resentful.

❧ On my flight back home, I had the same seat as on my flight out—aisle seat, first row of coach. There was a woman on the flight with a medical condition who needed two seats. A flight attendant asked if I would be willing to move to first class to accommodate this need. I quickly agreed. I got a big, comfortable leather seat, a soft drink, some snacks, a magazine and got to watch the movie for free!

❧ I couldn't believe it. I had wondered what it was like to sit in first class, and now I was experiencing it. The lunch meal was served on real plates with real silverware. After the meal, they brought warm, moist towels to wipe our hands and face. It was incredible!

❧ I began to think about my relationship with God. At times I feel that God is far away. I wonder what he's doing. I listen to people who talk about how much God is doing in their lives, and I'm jealous. I feel like I'm sitting in coach class, and I long to be in first class.

❧ God desires for us to have a "first-class" relationship with him. There should be no barriers between him and us. All we have to do is remove the curtain and approach him honestly. God desires that. Take the next 10 days to discover more about intimate communication with him.

appointments with god

____ psalm 4:1-3 God hears every prayer

____ psalm 139:23, 24 God knows your heart

____ matthew 6:5-15 Disciples taught to pray

____ matthew 7:7-11 God answers your prayers

____ luke 5:15, 16 Jesus' priority of prayer

____ ephesians 3:8-12 Approaching God

____ philippians 4:4-9 Talk to God about anything

____ 1 thessalonians 5:16-18 Constant prayer

____ 2 thessalonians 1:11, 12 Praying for friends

____ james 5:13-18 Powerful prayers

Today's Scripture: Psalm 4:1-3

The main thing I remember or learned from this Scripture is . . .

_____
_____
_____
_____
_____

Here is what God is trying to teach me through this Scripture . . .

_____
_____
_____
_____
_____
_____

As a result of this, today I will . . .

_____
_____
_____
_____
_____

Right now I need to pray about . . .

_____
_____
_____
_____
_____
_____

Today's Scripture: Psalm 139:23, 24

The main thing I remember or learned from this Scripture is . . .

_____

_____

_____

_____

_____

Here is what God is trying to teach me through this Scripture . . .

_____

_____

_____

_____

_____

As a result of this, today I will . . .

_____

_____

_____

_____

_____

Right now I need to pray about . . .

_____

_____

_____

_____

_____

appointments with god

Today's Scripture: Matthew 6:5-15

The main thing I remember or learned from this Scripture is . . .

_____

_____

_____

_____

_____

_____

Here is what God is trying to teach me through this Scripture . . .

_____

_____

_____

_____

_____

_____

_____

As a result of this, today I will . . .

_____

_____

_____

_____

_____

_____

Right now I need to pray about . . .

_____

_____

_____

_____

_____

_____

Today's Scripture: Matthew 7:7-11

The main thing I remember or learned from this Scripture is . . .

_____

_____

_____

_____

_____

_____

Here is what God is trying to teach me through this Scripture . . .

_____

_____

_____

_____

_____

_____

As a result of this, today I will . . .

_____

_____

_____

_____

_____

Right now I need to pray about . . .

_____

_____

_____

_____

_____

_____

appointments with god

Today's Scripture: Luke 5:15, 16
_____

The main thing I remember or learned from this Scripture is . . .
_____
_____
_____
_____
_____
_____

Here is what God is trying to teach me through this Scripture . . .
_____
_____
_____
_____
_____
_____
_____

As a result of this, today I will . . .
_____
_____
_____
_____
_____
_____
_____

Right now I need to pray about . . .
_____
_____
_____
_____
_____

Today's Scripture: Ephesians 3:8-12

The main thing I remember or learned from this Scripture is . . .

_____

_____

_____

_____

_____

Here is what God is trying to teach me through this Scripture . . .

_____

_____

_____

_____

_____

As a result of this, today I will . . .

_____

_____

_____

_____

_____

Right now I need to pray about . . .

_____

_____

_____

_____

_____

_____

appointments with god

Today's Scripture: Philippians 4:4-9

The main thing I remember or learned from this Scripture is . . .

_____

_____

_____

_____

_____

Here is what God is trying to teach me through this Scripture . . .

_____

_____

_____

_____

_____

As a result of this, today I will . . .

_____

_____

_____

_____

Right now I need to pray about . . .

_____

_____

_____

_____

_____

_____

Today's Scripture: 1 Thessalonians 5:16-18

The main thing I remember or learned from this Scripture is . . .

_____

_____

_____

_____

_____

Here is what God is trying to teach me through this Scripture . . .

_____

_____

_____

_____

_____

As a result of this, today I will . . .

_____

_____

_____

_____

_____

Right now I need to pray about . . .

_____

_____

_____

_____

_____

appointments with god

Today's Scripture: 2 Thessalonians 1:11, 12
_____

The main thing I remember or learned from this Scripture is . . .
_____
_____
_____
_____
_____
_____

Here is what God is trying to teach me through this Scripture . . .
_____
_____
_____
_____
_____
_____

As a result of this, today I will . . .
_____
_____
_____
_____
_____
_____

Right now I need to pray about . . .
_____
_____
_____
_____
_____
_____

Today's Scripture: James 5:13-18

The main thing I remember or learned from this Scripture is . . .

_____
_____
_____
_____
_____

Here is what God is trying to teach me through this Scripture . . .

_____
_____
_____
_____
_____
_____

As a result of this, today I will . . .

_____
_____
_____
_____
_____

Right now I need to pray about . . .

_____
_____
_____
_____
_____

appointments with god

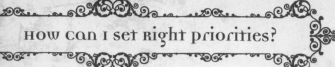

How can I set right priorities?

A few years ago I decided that I wanted to get into better shape. I made a resolution that I would begin running every day. I would drag myself out of bed at 6:30 each morning to jog. I have to be honest, it was pretty tough to do. In fact, most mornings I just wanted to stay in bed and sleep. But I kept it up for a few weeks.

❧ One of my friends who knew that I was running in the mornings told me about an upcoming race our city was going to have. It was a 10K race, 6.2 miles long. We decided to start training for it together. My friend showed up at my house at 6:30 every morning, and we started running together. I couldn't believe how much easier it was to get up to run knowing that my friend would be waiting for me and that we were training for a race. My whole perspective had changed. I actually started looking forward to getting up and running.

❧ Finally, the big day came, and my friend and I ran in the 10K race. He did much better than I did, but I set a personal best time! I couldn't believe it. After the race I thought about how much my priorities had changed. What had started out as an idea to get into better shape turned into a goal to compete in a race. It was amazing the difference that having a goal to work toward and having someone to train with had made in my motivation to run.

❧ Having the proper priorities in any part of your life can make all the difference in the world. The next 10 appointments with God will help you focus on having and keeping the proper priorities. So, what are you waiting for? Get off the couch and start running!

____ 2 Kings 18:1-8 Priorities rearranged

____ Proverbs 21:21 The secret of success

____ Matthew 6:25-34 No worries

____ Matthew 11:28-30 The need for rest

____ Luke 10:25-37 The greatest command

____ Luke 10:38-42 Time with God a priority

____ John 9:1-5 Using time wisely

____ Colossians 3:23, 24 A motto to live by

____ Hebrews 10:19-25 Time with believers a priority

____ James 2:14-26 Faith and good works

DATE: _____   **TIME:** _____ AM PM

Today's Scripture: 2 Kings 18:1-8

The main thing I remember or learned from this Scripture is . . .

_____

_____

_____

_____

_____

Here is what God is trying to teach me through this Scripture . . .

_____

_____

_____

_____

_____

As a result of this, today I will . . .

_____

_____

_____

_____

_____

Right now I need to pray about . . .

_____

_____

_____

_____

_____

_____

appointments with god

Today's Scripture: Proverbs 21:21

The main thing I remember or learned from this Scripture is . . .

_____

_____

_____

_____

_____

Here is what God is trying to teach me through this Scripture . . .

_____

_____

_____

_____

_____

_____

As a result of this, today I will . . .

_____

_____

_____

_____

_____

_____

Right now I need to pray about . . .

_____

_____

_____

_____

_____

Today's Scripture: Matthew 6:25-34

The main thing I remember or learned from this Scripture is . . .

_____

_____

_____

_____

_____

_____

Here is what God is trying to teach me through this Scripture . . .

_____

_____

_____

_____

_____

As a result of this, today I will . . .

_____

_____

_____

_____

_____

Right now I need to pray about . . .

_____

_____

_____

_____

_____

appointments with god

Today's Scripture: Matthew 11:28-30

The main thing I remember or learned from this Scripture is . . .

_____
_____
_____
_____
_____

Here is what God is trying to teach me through this Scripture . . .

_____
_____
_____
_____
_____
_____

As a result of this, today I will . . .

_____
_____
_____
_____
_____

Right now I need to pray about . . .

_____
_____
_____
_____
_____

Today's Scripture: Luke 10:25-37

The main thing I remember or learned from this Scripture is . . .

_____

_____

_____

_____

_____

Here is what God is trying to teach me through this Scripture . . .

_____

_____

_____

_____

_____

As a result of this, today I will . . .

_____

_____

_____

_____

_____

Right now I need to pray about . . .

_____

_____

_____

_____

_____

_____

appointments with god

Today's Scripture: Luke 10:38-42

The main thing I remember or learned from this Scripture is . . .

_____

_____

_____

_____

Here is what God is trying to teach me through this Scripture . . .

_____

_____

_____

_____

_____

As a result of this, today I will . . .

_____

_____

_____

_____

_____

Right now I need to pray about . . .

_____

_____

_____

_____

_____

Today's Scripture: John 9:1-5

The main thing I remember or learned from this Scripture is . . .

_____

_____

_____

_____

_____

Here is what God is trying to teach me through this Scripture . . .

_____

_____

_____

_____

_____

As a result of this, today I will . . .

_____

_____

_____

_____

_____

Right now I need to pray about . . .

_____

_____

_____

_____

_____

_____

appointments with god

Today's Scripture: Colossians 3:23, 24

The main thing I remember or learned from this Scripture is . . .

_____

_____

_____

_____

_____

_____

Here is what God is trying to teach me through this Scripture . . .

_____

_____

_____

_____

_____

_____

As a result of this, today I will . . .

_____

_____

_____

_____

_____

_____

Right now I need to pray about . . .

_____

_____

_____

_____

_____

Today's Scripture: Hebrews 10:19-25

The main thing I remember or learned from this Scripture is . . .

_____
_____
_____
_____
_____

Here is what God is trying to teach me through this Scripture . . .

_____
_____
_____
_____
_____

As a result of this, today I will . . .

_____
_____
_____
_____
_____

Right now I need to pray about . . .

_____
_____
_____
_____
_____

appointments with god

Today's Scripture: James 2:14-26

The main thing I remember or learned from this Scripture is . . .

_____

_____

_____

_____

_____

Here is what God is trying to teach me through this Scripture . . .

_____

_____

_____

_____

_____

As a result of this, today I will . . .

_____

_____

_____

_____

_____

Right now I need to pray about . . .

_____

_____

_____

_____

_____

how should i handle my stuff?

My wife and I just bought our first digital camera. We were waiting for the manufacturers to work out some of the bugs and also for the prices to go down. I did quite a bit of research about digital cameras. I shopped at all the electronics stores and talked to the sales people. I searched the Internet for the best camera at the best price.

❧ After all of the research, investigation and discussion with other digital camera owners, I bought one. I spent a little more money than I'd originally planned in order to get some added features. I bought extra memory for it and a cool little padded bag to carry it. The very first evening I had it, I sat at home and read through the entire owner's manual. I wanted to know everything this camera would do. I experimented by taking pictures around the house, transferring them to my computer and printing them out. I loved the results.

❧ Two days later, I took my camera outside to take some pictures of my daughter Morgan riding her bike. I put the camera in my pocket and began to run alongside her as she rode down the sidewalk. A few yards later, I heard a crash and saw my new digital camera bouncing behind me down the sidewalk! I raced back to pick it up. There were three big scratches on it from the concrete. I turned the camera on, and it worked. I was relieved. But those big, ugly scratches were still there. I was upset.

❧ When I went inside to put the camera away, I showed my wife. She responded, "Well, now you don't have to worry about scratching it anymore." I could hardly believe my ears. I had worked hard to get this camera. It cost a lot of money. And she thought a few scratches didn't matter? What was she thinking?

❧ To be honest, my wife has a better handle on possessions than I do. In your next 10 meetings with God and his Word, you'll see what the Bible says about handling your stuff. You might be surprised.

___ 2 kings 5:1, 9-18 The value of humility

___ 1 chronicles 29:10-17 God owns everything

___ ecclesiastes 5:10-16 Money never satisfies

___ mark 12:41-44 The greater gift

___ luke 16:1-15 Managing possessions

___ romans 13:7, 8 Repaying debts

___ 2 corinthians 9:6-11 Giving generously

___ 2 corinthians 9:12-15 Giving obediently

___ 1 timothy 6:3-10 The love of money

___ hebrews 13:5, 6 God better than money

Today's Scripture: 2 Kings 5:1, 9-18

The main thing I remember or learned from this Scripture is . . .

_____

_____

_____

_____

_____

Here is what God is trying to teach me through this Scripture . . .

_____

_____

_____

_____

_____

_____

As a result of this, today I will . . .

_____

_____

_____

_____

_____

Right now I need to pray about . . .

_____

_____

_____

_____

_____

Today's Scripture: 1 Chronicles 29:10-17

The main thing I remember or learned from this Scripture is . . .

_____

_____

_____

_____

_____

Here is what God is trying to teach me through this Scripture . . .

_____

_____

_____

_____

_____

As a result of this, today I will . . .

_____

_____

_____

_____

_____

Right now I need to pray about . . .

_____

_____

_____

_____

_____

_____

Today's Scripture: Ecclesiastes 5:10-16

The main thing I remember or learned from this Scripture is . . .

_____
_____
_____
_____
_____
_____

Here is what God is trying to teach me through this Scripture . . .

_____
_____
_____
_____
_____
_____
_____

As a result of this, today I will . . .

_____
_____
_____
_____
_____
_____

Right now I need to pray about . . .

_____
_____
_____
_____
_____
_____

Today's Scripture: Mark 12:41-44

The main thing I remember or learned from this Scripture is . . .

_____

_____

_____

_____

_____

_____

Here is what God is trying to teach me through this Scripture . . .

_____

_____

_____

_____

_____

As a result of this, today I will . . .

_____

_____

_____

_____

_____

Right now I need to pray about . . .

_____

_____

_____

_____

_____

_____

appointments with god

Today's Scripture: Luke 16:1-15

The main thing I remember or learned from this Scripture is . . .

_____

_____

_____

_____

_____

Here is what God is trying to teach me through this Scripture . . .

_____

_____

_____

_____

_____

As a result of this, today I will . . .

_____

_____

_____

_____

_____

Right now I need to pray about . . .

_____

_____

_____

_____

_____

MY WORLD ❖ ENCOUNTERS 41-50

Today's Scripture: Romans 13:7, 8

The main thing I remember or learned from this Scripture is . . .

_____

_____

_____

_____

_____

_____

Here is what God is trying to teach me through this Scripture . . .

_____

_____

_____

_____

_____

_____

As a result of this, today I will . . .

_____

_____

_____

_____

_____

_____

Right now I need to pray about . . .

_____

_____

_____

_____

_____

_____

appointments with god

Today's Scripture: 2 Corinthians 9:6-11

The main thing I remember or learned from this Scripture is . . .

_____
_____
_____
_____
_____

Here is what God is trying to teach me through this Scripture . . .

_____
_____
_____
_____
_____
_____

As a result of this, today I will . . .

_____
_____
_____
_____
_____

Right now I need to pray about . . .

_____
_____
_____
_____
_____

Today's Scripture: 2 Corinthians 9:12-15

The main thing I remember or learned from this Scripture is . . .

_____

_____

_____

_____

_____

Here is what God is trying to teach me through this Scripture . . .

_____

_____

_____

_____

_____

As a result of this, today I will . . .

_____

_____

_____

_____

_____

Right now I need to pray about . . .

_____

_____

_____

_____

_____

appointments with god

Today's Scripture: 1 Timothy 6:3-10

The main thing I remember or learned from this Scripture is . . .

_____

_____

_____

_____

_____

Here is what God is trying to teach me through this Scripture . . .

_____

_____

_____

_____

_____

_____

_____

As a result of this, today I will . . .

_____

_____

_____

_____

_____

_____

Right now I need to pray about . . .

_____

_____

_____

_____

_____

_____

Today's Scripture: Hebrews 13:5, 6
_____

The main thing I remember or learned from this Scripture is . . .
_____
_____
_____
_____
_____
_____

Here is what God is trying to teach me through this Scripture . . .
_____
_____
_____
_____
_____
_____

As a result of this, today I will . . .
_____
_____
_____
_____
_____
_____

Right now I need to pray about . . .
_____
_____
_____
_____
_____
_____

appointments with god

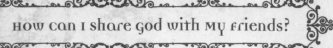

how can I share god with my friends?

When someone talks about *witnessing* to others, what do you think of? Someone standing on a street corner, holding a sign and shouting, "Repent! The end is near!"? Someone handing out Christian tracts at the mall? Someone who has a Christian bumper sticker or fish magnet on his car? Just what is witnessing all about? And why does it seem so difficult?

❖ Simply put, witnessing is sharing with others what God means to you. I'm not the kind of guy who stands on top of the lunch table and shouts to everyone that they are going to Hell unless they turn to God. I tend to be more like the apostle Andrew. In John 1:35-42 Andrew met Jesus and got to spend an entire day with him. As soon as he left Jesus, he found his brother Peter and told him about his time with the Messiah. Then Andrew brought Peter to meet Jesus.

❖ I'll never forget the first person I helped introduce to Jesus. Jimmy Rivers and I were in the fourth grade together. As we rode our bikes in the parking lot of a Catholic church in our neighborhood, I asked Jimmy where he went to church. He said that he went to that particular church—when he and his family went, only a couple of times a year, usually around Christmas.

❖ I told Jimmy that I went to church almost every Sunday. He began asking me a lot of questions about church, God and Heaven. I answered as many questions as I could, but I didn't know all the answers. Later we rode over to my house, and I gave Jimmy one of my Bibles.

❖ A few days later Jimmy asked if he could come to church with me. I didn't have an elaborate witnessing plan—I just talked about what God meant to me. I wasn't a paid minister—I was just a fourth grader. I didn't have all the answers—I just told him what I knew. A few months later Jimmy and his entire family became Christians.

❖ As you read the next few appointments with God, I hope you'll see that sharing God with your friends doesn't have to be scary or painful.

Today's Scripture: Jonah 3:1-10

The main thing I remember or learned from this Scripture is . . .

_____

_____

_____

_____

_____

Here is what God is trying to teach me through this Scripture . . .

_____

_____

_____

_____

_____

As a result of this, today I will . . .

_____

_____

_____

_____

_____

Right now I need to pray about . . .

_____

_____

_____

_____

_____

_____

appointments with god

Today's Scripture: Matthew 5:13-16

The main thing I remember or learned from this Scripture is . . .

_____

_____

_____

_____

_____

Here is what God is trying to teach me through this Scripture . . .

_____

_____

_____

_____

_____

As a result of this, today I will . . .

_____

_____

_____

_____

_____

Right now I need to pray about . . .

_____

_____

_____

_____

_____

DATE: _____ TIME: _____ AM PM

Today's Scripture: Mark 5:1-20

The main thing I remember or learned from this Scripture is . . .

_____
_____
_____
_____
_____

Here is what God is trying to teach me through this Scripture . . .

_____
_____
_____
_____
_____

As a result of this, today I will . . .

_____
_____
_____
_____
_____

Right now I need to pray about . . .

_____
_____
_____
_____
_____
_____

Today's Scripture: Acts 1:8

The main thing I remember or learned from this Scripture is . . .

_____

_____

_____

_____

_____

Here is what God is trying to teach me through this Scripture . . .

_____

_____

_____

_____

_____

_____

_____

As a result of this, today I will . . .

_____

_____

_____

_____

_____

Right now I need to pray about . . .

_____

_____

_____

_____

_____

Today's Scripture: Acts 4:8-22
_____

The main thing I remember or learned from this Scripture is . . .
_____
_____
_____
_____
_____
_____

Here is what God is trying to teach me through this Scripture . . .
_____
_____
_____
_____
_____
_____

As a result of this, today I will . . .
_____
_____
_____
_____
_____
_____

Right now I need to pray about . . .
_____
_____
_____
_____
_____
_____

appointments with god

Today's Scripture: Colossians 4:2-6

The main thing I remember or learned from this Scripture is . . .

_____

_____

_____

_____

_____

Here is what God is trying to teach me through this Scripture . . .

_____

_____

_____

_____

_____

As a result of this, today I will . . .

_____

_____

_____

_____

_____

Right now I need to pray about . . .

_____

_____

_____

_____

_____

_____

Today's Scripture: 1 Thessalonians 2:4-12 _____

The main thing I remember or learned from this Scripture is . . . _____

_____

_____

_____

_____

_____

Here is what God is trying to teach me through this Scripture . . . _____

_____

_____

_____

_____

_____

As a result of this, today I will . . . _____

_____

_____

_____

_____

Right now I need to pray about . . . _____

_____

_____

_____

_____

_____

_____

Today's Scripture: Philemon 4-7

The main thing I remember or learned from this Scripture is . . .

_____

_____

_____

_____

_____

Here is what God is trying to teach me through this Scripture . . .

_____

_____

_____

_____

_____

_____

As a result of this, today I will . . .

_____

_____

_____

_____

_____

_____

Right now I need to pray about . . .

_____

_____

_____

_____

_____

Today's Scripture: James 1:26, 27

The main thing I remember or learned from this Scripture is . . .

_____

_____

_____

_____

_____

Here is what God is trying to teach me through this Scripture . . .

_____

_____

_____

_____

_____

_____

As a result of this, today I will . . .

_____

_____

_____

_____

_____

_____

Right now I need to pray about . . .

_____

_____

_____

_____

_____

_____

appointments with god

DATE: _____   TIME: _____ AM PM

Today's Scripture: 1 Peter 3:15, 16 _____

The main thing I remember or learned from this Scripture is . . .

_____

_____

_____

_____

_____

Here is what God is trying to teach me through this Scripture . . .

_____

_____

_____

_____

_____

As a result of this, today I will . . .

_____

_____

_____

_____

_____

Right now I need to pray about . . .

_____

_____

_____

_____

_____

How can I be a good friend?

Two weeks before I went into junior high school, my parents informed me that we were moving from our home in New York to Missouri. I couldn't believe this was happening. What about my friends and all the plans we'd made? What about the soccer team I would leave behind? I was devastated and didn't want to move. I'll never forget saying good-bye to my friends and making the long drive to Missouri.

❧ On the first day of junior high school, I woke up with a stomachache. I was so nervous about going to a new school where I didn't know anyone. I wouldn't have any friends. I didn't want to be the new kid. I wanted to go back to New York.

❧ That first morning, I was the first one picked up by the bus. As it filled up, it seemed that everyone knew everyone else—but no one knew me. When we arrived at the school, I made my way to my assigned locker. I smiled and nodded at a few kids, but didn't see anyone I knew.

❧ At my locker, I put my books and things inside. I dreaded walking into the first class. The teacher probably would have everyone stand up and introduce themselves—then everyone would know I was the new kid. I said a quick prayer, took a breath and closed the locker door. Standing right next to me, at his locker, was a guy I'd never seen before. He said, "Hi! My name's Dennis." I introduced myself. He thought it was cool that I had just moved from New York. When he found out that we had the same first hour, he said something that caught me off guard. "Can I introduce you to some of my friends in that same class?" Wow! This guy thought it was cool that I was from New York, and, actually, wanted to introduce me to his friends.

❧ Dennis and I became best friends all through high school. Sometimes being a good friend is as simple as just introducing yourself to someone you don't know. Sometimes it's a whole lot more. The next 10 encounters in the Word will give you some practical tips for being a good friend.

____ genesis 14:8-16 Friends help in tough times

____ exodus 32:1-14 When friends are in trouble

____ 1 samuel 20:1-3, 30-42 Protecting friends from harm

____ 2 samuel 19:31-33 Friends care for each other

____ proverbs 13:14, 20 Choosing friends wisely

____ proverbs 17:17 A friend always loves

____ matthew 18:21-35 The importance of forgiveness

____ john 15:12-17 Jesus shows his friendship

____ acts 9:20-25 Saul rescued by friends

____ 2 corinthians 5:18-20 God's ambassadors

Today's Scripture: Genesis 14:8-16

The main thing I remember or learned from this Scripture is . . .

_____
_____
_____
_____
_____

Here is what God is trying to teach me through this Scripture . . .

_____
_____
_____
_____
_____
_____

As a result of this, today I will . . .

_____
_____
_____
_____
_____
_____

Right now I need to pray about . . .

_____
_____
_____
_____
_____

Today's Scripture: Exodus 32:1-14

The main thing I remember or learned from this Scripture is . . .

_____
_____
_____
_____
_____
_____

Here is what God is trying to teach me through this Scripture . . .

_____
_____
_____
_____
_____

As a result of this, today I will . . .

_____
_____
_____
_____
_____

Right now I need to pray about . . .

_____
_____
_____
_____
_____
_____

appointments with god

Today's Scripture: 1 Samuel 20:1-3, 30-42

The main thing I remember or learned from this Scripture is . . .

_____

_____

_____

_____

_____

Here is what God is trying to teach me through this Scripture . . .

_____

_____

_____

_____

_____

As a result of this, today I will . . .

_____

_____

_____

_____

_____

Right now I need to pray about . . .

_____

_____

_____

_____

_____

Today's Scripture: 2 Samuel 19:31-33

The main thing I remember or learned from this Scripture is . . .

_____

_____

_____

_____

Here is what God is trying to teach me through this Scripture . . .

_____

_____

_____

_____

As a result of this, today I will . . .

_____

_____

_____

_____

Right now I need to pray about . . .

_____

_____

_____

_____

_____

appointments with god

Today's Scripture: Proverbs 13:14, 20

The main thing I remember or learned from this Scripture is . . .

_____
_____
_____
_____
_____

Here is what God is trying to teach me through this Scripture . . .

_____
_____
_____
_____
_____
_____

As a result of this, today I will . . .

_____
_____
_____
_____
_____
_____

Right now I need to pray about . . .

_____
_____
_____
_____
_____

Today's Scripture: Proverbs 17:17

The main thing I remember or learned from this Scripture is . . .

_____

_____

_____

_____

_____

_____

Here is what God is trying to teach me through this Scripture . . .

_____

_____

_____

_____

_____

As a result of this, today I will . . .

_____

_____

_____

_____

Right now I need to pray about . . .

_____

_____

_____

_____

_____

appointments with god

Today's Scripture: Matthew 18:21-35

The main thing I remember or learned from this Scripture is . . .

_____

_____

_____

_____

Here is what God is trying to teach me through this Scripture . . .

_____

_____

_____

_____

_____

As a result of this, today I will . . .

_____

_____

_____

_____

Right now I need to pray about . . .

_____

_____

_____

_____

_____

Today's Scripture: John 15:12-17

The main thing I remember or learned from this Scripture is . . .

_____

_____

_____

_____

_____

Here is what God is trying to teach me through this Scripture . . .

_____

_____

_____

_____

_____

As a result of this, today I will . . .

_____

_____

_____

_____

_____

Right now I need to pray about . . .

_____

_____

_____

_____

_____

appointments with god

Today's Scripture: Acts 9:20-25

The main thing I remember or learned from this Scripture is . . .

_____
_____
_____
_____
_____
_____

Here is what God is trying to teach me through this Scripture . . .

_____
_____
_____
_____
_____
_____
_____

As a result of this, today I will . . .

_____
_____
_____
_____
_____
_____
_____

Right now I need to pray about . . .

_____
_____
_____
_____
_____
_____

Today's Scripture: 2 Corinthians 5:18-20
_____

The main thing I remember or learned from this Scripture is . . .
_____
_____
_____
_____
_____
_____

Here is what God is trying to teach me through this Scripture . . .
_____
_____
_____
_____
_____
_____

As a result of this, today I will . . .
_____
_____
_____
_____
_____
_____

Right now I need to pray about . . .
_____
_____
_____
_____
_____
_____

appointments with god

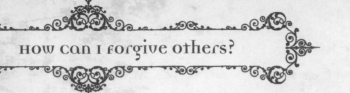

U nless you're a hermit living in a cave somewhere, the need for forgiveness is something you have undoubtedly encountered more than once. Over the past few months, I've had to forgive one person for gossiping about me, someone else lied to me and still another person stole something from me. Forgiveness is an issue that we deal with quite often.

❧ Which is tougher to do? Is it harder to seek forgiveness from someone or to extend forgiveness to someone who needs it from you? I think it all depends on the situation. Asking for forgiveness is definitely harder for me, in the short term. It requires that I humble myself, go to the person I've hurt and lay it all out for the person, hoping he offers me forgiveness. Once that happens, it's all good!

❧ On the other hand, forgiving someone else may be easier at first, but can be hard to stick to over the long haul. If someone has wronged me, and he comes to me and asks for forgiveness, chances are I will say that I forgive him. But many times I don't treat that person as if I've totally forgiven him. I may hold a grudge against him, consciously or subconsciously. I watch his every move. I make sure that he isn't in a position to hurt me again. And sometimes when I'm cutting the grass or watching TV I might start thinking about the situation and get angry at him all over again. I guess I'm better at saying "I forgive" than I am about feeling and acting as if I've forgiven.

❧ If you're like me, you'll benefit greatly from this section of appointments about forgiving others. Jesus said some pretty tough stuff on the topic.

Today's Scripture: Genesis 45:1-15

The main thing I remember or learned from this Scripture is . . .

_____
_____
_____
_____
_____

Here is what God is trying to teach me through this Scripture . . .

_____
_____
_____
_____
_____

As a result of this, today I will . . .

_____
_____
_____
_____
_____

Right now I need to pray about . . .

_____
_____
_____
_____
_____
_____

Today's Scripture: Matthew 5:10-12

The main thing I remember or learned from this Scripture is . . .

_____

_____

_____

_____

_____

Here is what God is trying to teach me through this Scripture . . .

_____

_____

_____

_____

_____

_____

_____

As a result of this, today I will . . .

_____

_____

_____

_____

_____

_____

Right now I need to pray about . . .

_____

_____

_____

_____

_____

DATE: _____ TIME: _____ AM PM

Today's Scripture: Matthew 12:30-32

The main thing I remember or learned from this Scripture is . . .

_____
_____
_____
_____
_____
_____

Here is what God is trying to teach me through this Scripture . . .

_____
_____
_____
_____
_____
_____

As a result of this, today I will

_____
_____
_____
_____
_____
_____

Right now I need to pray about . . .

_____
_____
_____
_____
_____

Today's Scripture: Matthew 18:15-19

The main thing I remember or learned from this Scripture is . . .

_____

_____

_____

_____

_____

_____

Here is what God is trying to teach me through this Scripture . . .

_____

_____

_____

_____

_____

_____

_____

As a result of this, today I will . . .

_____

_____

_____

_____

_____

_____

Right now I need to pray about . . .

_____

_____

_____

_____

_____

_____

Today's Scripture: Mark 11:23-25

The main thing I remember or learned from this Scripture is . . .

_____

_____

_____

_____

_____

_____

Here is what God is trying to teach me through this Scripture . . .

_____

_____

_____

_____

_____

_____

As a result of this, today I will . . .

_____

_____

_____

_____

_____

_____

Right now I need to pray about . . .

_____

_____

_____

_____

_____

_____

appointments with god

Today's Scripture: Luke 6:37, 38

The main thing I remember or learned from this Scripture is . . .

_____

_____

_____

_____

_____

Here is what God is trying to teach me through this Scripture . . .

_____

_____

_____

_____

_____

_____

As a result of this, today I will . . .

_____

_____

_____

_____

_____

_____

Right now I need to pray about . . .

_____

_____

_____

_____

_____

Today's Scripture: Luke 17:3, 4

The main thing I remember or learned from this Scripture is . . .

_____

_____

_____

_____

_____

Here is what God is trying to teach me through this Scripture . . .

_____

_____

_____

_____

_____

As a result of this, today I will . . .

_____

_____

_____

_____

_____

Right now I need to pray about . . .

_____

_____

_____

_____

_____

_____

appointments with god

Today's Scripture: Luke 23:32-43

The main thing I remember or learned from this Scripture is . . .

_____

_____

_____

_____

_____

_____

Here is what God is trying to teach me through this Scripture . . .

_____

_____

_____

_____

_____

_____

As a result of this, today I will . . .

_____

_____

_____

_____

_____

_____

Right now I need to pray about . . .

_____

_____

_____

_____

_____

Today's Scripture: John 8:1-11
_____

The main thing I remember or learned from this Scripture is . . .
_____
_____
_____
_____
_____

Here is what God is trying to teach me through this Scripture . . .
_____
_____
_____
_____
_____
_____
_____

As a result of this, today I will . . .
_____
_____
_____
_____
_____

Right now I need to pray about . . .
_____
_____
_____
_____
_____
_____

appointments with god

Today's Scripture: Colossians 3:12-14
_____

The main thing I remember or learned from this Scripture is . . .
_____
_____
_____
_____
_____
_____

Here is what God is trying to teach me through this Scripture . . .
_____
_____
_____
_____
_____
_____
_____

As a result of this, today I will . . .
_____
_____
_____
_____
_____
_____

Right now I need to pray about . . .
_____
_____
_____
_____
_____
_____

How can I serve others?

Several years ago our church sponsored an all-night New Year's Eve party for junior high youth. The night was filled with pizza, video games, prizes, a midnight countdown and tons of kids. It was an incredible experience. After we served breakfast, a group of eighth graders and I helped clean up the food area. Someone had spilled a gallon of milk. Travis, one of the teens, grabbed a sponge, got underneath a table and began to wipe it up. Maggie, another eighth grader who was standing next to me, commented, "Someday I hope that I marry a guy who's not afraid to clean up spilled milk." Not only did she think he was cute, she also admired his willingness to serve others.

❦ The all-night affair ended a few hours later, but I couldn't help but be impressed that Travis would jump in and help clean up. Most teens his age wouldn't volunteer to clean their own rooms, much less someone else's warm, smelly, spilled milk. But Travis did it without even being asked. I was pleased also that Maggie had noticed his act of service. Many people think only of themselves, and never think to encourage others when they do something nice.

❦ Fast-forward eight years. I had the privilege of performing Travis's wedding ceremony. You've probably guessed it by now—his bride was Maggie. Who would have guessed that a simple act of service years before would lead to their getting married?

❦ The world could be divided into two different kinds of people: those who help others and those who help only themselves. Your next 10 encounters in the Word provide some great instruction on the priority of serving others. Medical missionary and humanitarian Albert Schweitzer said, "I don't know what your destiny will be, but one thing I know: the only ones among you who will be really happy are those who will have sought and found how to serve." You never know who might be watching.

____ Matthew 20:25-28 Jesus' challenge

____ Luke 1:26-38 A willing servant

____ Luke 17:7-10 A serving attitude

____ Luke 22:24-26 Greatness in God's eyes

____ John 13:3-17 A supreme example

____ 1 Corinthians 15:58 Fully devoted to God

____ Galatians 5:13, 14 Serving in love

____ Ephesians 2:8-10 Prepared to do good

____ 2 Thessalonians 3:11-13 Never stop serving

____ 1 Peter 4:8-11 Gifted for service

Today's Scripture: Matthew 20:25-28

The main thing I remember or learned from this Scripture is . . .

_____

_____

_____

_____

_____

Here is what God is trying to teach me through this Scripture . . .

_____

_____

_____

_____

_____

_____

As a result of this, today I will . . .

_____

_____

_____

_____

_____

_____

Right now I need to pray about . . .

_____

_____

_____

_____

_____

_____

DATE: _____ TIME: _____ AM PM

Today's Scripture: Luke 1:26-38
_____

The main thing I remember or learned from this Scripture is . . .
_____
_____
_____
_____
_____

Here is what God is trying to teach me through this Scripture . . .
_____
_____
_____
_____
_____

As a result of this, today I will . . .
_____
_____
_____
_____
_____

Right now I need to pray about . . .
_____
_____
_____
_____
_____

appointments with god

Today's Scripture: Luke 17:7-10

The main thing I remember or learned from this Scripture is . . .

_____

_____

_____

_____

_____

Here is what God is trying to teach me through this Scripture . . .

_____

_____

_____

_____

_____

_____

As a result of this, today I will . . .

_____

_____

_____

_____

_____

Right now I need to pray about . . .

_____

_____

_____

_____

_____

Today's Scripture: Luke 22:24-26

The main thing I remember or learned from this Scripture is . . .

_____

_____

_____

_____

_____

Here is what God is trying to teach me through this Scripture . . .

_____

_____

_____

_____

_____

As a result of this, today I will . . .

_____

_____

_____

_____

Right now I need to pray about . . .

_____

_____

_____

_____

appointments with god

Today's Scripture: John 13:3-17

The main thing I remember or learned from this Scripture is . . .

_____

_____

_____

_____

Here is what God is trying to teach me through this Scripture . . .

_____

_____

_____

_____

_____

As a result of this, today I will . . .

_____

_____

_____

_____

_____

Right now I need to pray about . . .

_____

_____

_____

_____

_____

Today's Scripture: 1 Corinthians 15:58 _____

The main thing I remember or learned from this Scripture is . . . _____

_____

_____

_____

_____

_____

Here is what God is trying to teach me through this Scripture . . . _____

_____

_____

_____

_____

_____

As a result of this, today I will . . . _____

_____

_____

_____

_____

Right now I need to pray about . . . _____

_____

_____

_____

_____

_____

Today's Scripture: Galatians 5:13, 14

The main thing I remember or learned from this Scripture is . . .

_____

_____

_____

_____

Here is what God is trying to teach me through this Scripture . . .

_____

_____

_____

_____

_____

As a result of this, today I will . . .

_____

_____

_____

_____

_____

Right now I need to pray about . . .

_____

_____

_____

_____

_____

Today's Scripture: Ephesians 2:8-10

The main thing I remember or learned from this Scripture is . . .

_____

_____

_____

_____

_____

Here is what God is trying to teach me through this Scripture . . .

_____

_____

_____

_____

_____

As a result of this, today I will . . .

_____

_____

_____

_____

_____

Right now I need to pray about . . .

_____

_____

_____

_____

_____

appointments with god

Today's Scripture: 2 Thessalonians 3:11-13

The main thing I remember or learned from this Scripture is . . .

_____

_____

_____

_____

_____

Here is what God is trying to teach me through this Scripture . . .

_____

_____

_____

_____

_____

As a result of this, today I will . . .

_____

_____

_____

_____

_____

Right now I need to pray about . . .

_____

_____

_____

_____

_____

Today's Scripture: 1 Peter 4:8-11

The main thing I remember or learned from this Scripture is . . .

_____

_____

_____

_____

_____

Here is what God is trying to teach me through this Scripture . . .

_____

_____

_____

_____

_____

As a result of this, today I will . . .

_____

_____

_____

_____

_____

Right now I need to pray about . . .

_____

_____

_____

_____

_____

_____

appointments with god

what is true love?

Most people grow up with questions about love. "Will I get married?" "Will I stay married?" "How will I know who is 'the one' for me?" "What is true love?"

❧ Years ago a youth minister friend of mine spoke on the topic of "true love" at a youth group retreat in California. During one session of the weekend, my friend challenged the teens to keep themselves sexually pure until marriage. After speaking on the benefits of abstinence, he led a commitment time. The youth had the opportunity to sign a card, promising they would stay sexually pure until their wedding night.

❧ Out of the 30 young adults who attended, only a handful chose to make that commitment. My friend was disappointed because he had put his heart and soul into the retreat. So he did something I couldn't believe. He gave a $100 check to each teen who signed the commitment card! He filled the check out completely, except he didn't sign it. He told the students that if they kept their promise, he'd sign the check when they got married, and they would get $100.

❧ Several years later my friend was speaking at a youth convention when a young lady came up to him. She looked vaguely familiar. She told him she had been at the retreat where he had spoken and had made the commitment to stay sexually pure. She showed him her wedding ring. She thanked him for helping her make the commitment and said that she had kept it, even though it was hard to do. Then she pulled that old check out of her Bible. My friend said that he was never so glad to give someone $100.

❧ Before the girl walked away, she asked if it would be OK if she took the $100 and used it with the youth group that she was now leading. She wanted to help her teens make the same commitment.

❧ During these next 10 days, you will not have all your questions about love answered, but you will see God's perspective on this topic. After all, he created love and has an incredible plan for your life!

____ Matthew 22:39, 40 A great rule to follow   ____ Ephesians 5:21-33 Marital love

____ John 13:34, 35 Known by our love   ____ 1 Thessalonians 4:3-8 Living a pure life

____ John 14:15-21 Loving obedience   ____ Hebrews 13:4 To love and to cherish

____ 1 Corinthians 6:18-20 Bought with a price   ____ 1 John 3:16, 17 Real love demonstrated

____ 1 Corinthians 13:4-13 True love described   ____ 1 John 4:7-21 True love defined

Today's Scripture: Matthew 22:39, 40

The main thing I remember or learned from this Scripture is . . .

_____

_____

_____

_____

_____

Here is what God is trying to teach me through this Scripture . . .

_____

_____

_____

_____

_____

As a result of this, today I will . . .

_____

_____

_____

_____

Right now I need to pray about . . .

_____

_____

_____

_____

_____

appointments with god

Today's Scripture: John 13:34, 35
_____

The main thing I remember or learned from this Scripture is . . .
_____
_____
_____
_____
_____

Here is what God is trying to teach me through this Scripture . . .
_____
_____
_____
_____
_____
_____

As a result of this, today I will . . .
_____
_____
_____
_____
_____
_____

Right now I need to pray about . . .
_____
_____
_____
_____
_____
_____

MY WORLD ❖ ENCOUNTERS 91-100

Today's Scripture: John 14:15-21

The main thing I remember or learned from this Scripture is . . .

_____
_____
_____
_____
_____
_____

Here is what God is trying to teach me through this Scripture . . .

_____
_____
_____
_____
_____
_____

As a result of this, today I will . . .

_____
_____
_____
_____
_____
_____

Right now I need to pray about . . .

_____
_____
_____
_____
_____
_____

Today's Scripture: 1 Corinthians 6:18-20

The main thing I remember or learned from this Scripture is . . .

_____

_____

_____

_____

_____

Here is what God is trying to teach me through this Scripture . . .

_____

_____

_____

_____

_____

As a result of this, today I will . . .

_____

_____

_____

_____

_____

Right now I need to pray about . . .

_____

_____

_____

_____

_____

Today's Scripture: 1 Corinthians 13:4-13

The main thing I remember or learned from this Scripture is . . .

_____
_____
_____
_____
_____

Here is what God is trying to teach me through this Scripture . . .

_____
_____
_____
_____
_____
_____

As a result of this, today I will . . .

_____
_____
_____
_____
_____
_____

Right now I need to pray about . . .

_____
_____
_____
_____
_____
_____

appointments with god

Today's Scripture: Ephesians 5:21-33

The main thing I remember or learned from this Scripture is . . .

_____

_____

_____

_____

_____

Here is what God is trying to teach me through this Scripture . . .

_____

_____

_____

_____

_____

_____

As a result of this, today I will . . .

_____

_____

_____

_____

_____

Right now I need to pray about . . .

_____

_____

_____

_____

_____

Today's Scripture: 1 Thessalonians 4:3-8

The main thing I remember or learned from this Scripture is . . .

_____

_____

_____

_____

_____

_____

Here is what God is trying to teach me through this Scripture . . .

_____

_____

_____

_____

_____

As a result of this, today I will . . .

_____

_____

_____

_____

_____

Right now I need to pray about . . .

_____

_____

_____

_____

_____

appointments with god

Today's Scripture: Hebrews 13:4
_____

The main thing I remember or learned from this Scripture is . . .
_____
_____
_____
_____
_____

Here is what God is trying to teach me through this Scripture . . .
_____
_____
_____
_____
_____
_____

As a result of this, today I will . . .
_____
_____
_____
_____
_____

Right now I need to pray about . . .
_____
_____
_____
_____
_____

DATE: _____ TIME: _____ AM PM

Today's Scripture: 1 John 3:16, 17

The main thing I remember or learned from this Scripture is . . .

_____
_____
_____
_____
_____

Here is what God is trying to teach me through this Scripture . . .

_____
_____
_____
_____
_____

As a result of this, today I will . . .

_____
_____
_____
_____
_____

Right now I need to pray about . . .

_____
_____
_____
_____
_____

Today's Scripture: 1 John 4:7-21

The main thing I remember or learned from this Scripture is . . .

_____

_____

_____

_____

_____

Here is what God is trying to teach me through this Scripture . . .

_____

_____

_____

_____

_____

_____

As a result of this, today I will . . .

_____

_____

_____

_____

_____

Right now I need to pray about . . .

_____

_____

_____

_____

_____

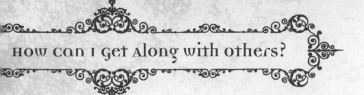

Do you know the difference between dogs and cats? A dog says, "You feed me, pet me, walk me, play with me and love me—you must be God." A cat says, "You feed me, pet me, walk me, play with me and love me—*I* must be God!" As funny as that sounds, even dog and cat owners would admit it's pretty true. I think that, in the human world, there are people who could be classified as "dogs" or "cats." There are certain people whom everyone wants to be around. Everybody wants to befriend them. They're positive, encouraging and lots of fun. But there are also people who believe that everyone else exists to take care of them. They think that the world revolves around their every thought, need and desire. Almost no one wants to be around this kind of person.

❋ I have some great friends, with whom I go out and eat, watch sports or just have fun. I have some great memories of times together with them. Often when we get together, the conversation turns to a funny story that happened some time ago. And even though all of us were there, we relive the story time and again.

❋ I also have one or two people in my life who drive me crazy. Life seems to owe them everything, and they're always complaining about how awful something is. It seems as though God must have put them in my life with this challenge: "I dare you to love them." After being with these people, I can't wait to get away and talk to someone who is more positive.

❋ Being a good friend means that I need to treat all my friends with respect, not just those with whom I get along well. It also means that if I have a friend who is going through a tough time, I stick with him, rather than turn my back on him when he needs me most. These 10 appointments with God should stimulate some thoughts in your quest to be a good friend.

Today's Scripture: 1 Kings 21:4-10

The main thing I remember or learned from this Scripture is . . .

_____

_____

_____

_____

_____

Here is what God is trying to teach me through this Scripture . . .

_____

_____

_____

_____

_____

_____

_____

As a result of this, today I will . . .

_____

_____

_____

_____

_____

_____

Right now I need to pray about . . .

_____

_____

_____

_____

_____

_____

DATE: _____   TIME: _____ AM PM

Today's Scripture: Psalm 141:3-5

The main thing I remember or learned from this Scripture is . . .

_____

_____

_____

_____

_____

Here is what God is trying to teach me through this Scripture . . .

_____

_____

_____

_____

_____

As a result of this, today I will . . .

_____

_____

_____

_____

_____

Right now I need to pray about . . .

_____

_____

_____

_____

_____

Today's Scripture: Proverbs 29:1, 23

The main thing I remember or learned from this Scripture is . . .

_____
_____
_____
_____
_____
_____

Here is what God is trying to teach me through this Scripture . . .

_____
_____
_____
_____
_____
_____

As a result of this, today I will . . .

_____
_____
_____
_____
_____
_____

Right now I need to pray about . . .

_____
_____
_____
_____
_____

Today's Scripture: Matthew 5:33-37

The main thing I remember or learned from this Scripture is . . .

_____

_____

_____

_____

_____

Here is what God is trying to teach me through this Scripture . . .

_____

_____

_____

_____

_____

As a result of this, today I will . . .

_____

_____

_____

_____

_____

Right now I need to pray about . . .

_____

_____

_____

_____

_____

appointments with god

Today's Scripture: Matthew 5:43-48

The main thing I remember or learned from this Scripture is . . .

_____

_____

_____

_____

_____

Here is what God is trying to teach me through this Scripture . . .

_____

_____

_____

_____

_____

As a result of this, today I will . . .

_____

_____

_____

_____

_____

Right now I need to pray about . . .

_____

_____

_____

_____

_____

MY WORLD ❖ ENCOUNTERS 101-110

Today's Scripture: Romans 12:9-21 _____

The main thing I remember or learned from this Scripture is . . .

_____
_____
_____
_____
_____
_____

Here is what God is trying to teach me through this Scripture . . .

_____
_____
_____
_____
_____

As a result of this, today I will . . .

_____
_____
_____
_____
_____

Right now I need to pray about . . .

_____
_____
_____
_____
_____

appointments with god

Today's Scripture: Galatians 5:16-25

The main thing I remember or learned from this Scripture is . . .

_____

_____

_____

_____

_____

_____

Here is what God is trying to teach me through this Scripture . . .

_____

_____

_____

_____

_____

_____

_____

As a result of this, today I will . . .

_____

_____

_____

_____

_____

Right now I need to pray about . . .

_____

_____

_____

_____

_____

_____

Today's Scripture: Philippians 2:14-16

The main thing I remember or learned from this Scripture is . . .

_____

_____

_____

_____

_____

Here is what God is trying to teach me through this Scripture . . .

_____

_____

_____

_____

_____

As a result of this, today I will . . .

_____

_____

_____

_____

Right now I need to pray about . . .

_____

_____

_____

_____

_____

appointments with god

Today's Scripture: 1 Timothy 5:3-8

The main thing I remember or learned from this Scripture is . . .

_____

_____

_____

_____

_____

Here is what God is trying to teach me through this Scripture . . .

_____

_____

_____

_____

_____

As a result of this, today I will . . .

_____

_____

_____

_____

_____

_____

Right now I need to pray about . . .

_____

_____

_____

_____

_____

_____

Today's Scripture: 2 Peter 1:5-9

The main thing I remember or learned from this Scripture is . . .

_____

_____

_____

_____

_____

Here is what God is trying to teach me through this Scripture . . .

_____

_____

_____

_____

_____

_____

As a result of this, today I will . . .

_____

_____

_____

_____

_____

Right now I need to pray about . . .

_____

_____

_____

_____

_____

appointments with god

Do you ever feel as if your parents don't understand you? Like, about every other day? Have you ever gotten into an argument with your brother or sister? Anyone living in a family deals with conflict on a regular basis. Read a letter that I received from a girl who was in our church youth group:

Dear Michael,
I've got to be honest with you, sometimes I think that my life really stinks. When I was 7 my stepfather sexually abused me. I felt worthless and dirty. I tried to kill myself when I was 11 because I didn't want to live anymore. My mom and stepdad got a divorce last year, so I don't see him very often. Up until last night I didn't think that my mom cared for me at all. She didn't ever seem to notice that I was alive. I tried to talk with her, but she was always busy reading the paper or else she'd end up yelling at me. Last night I'd had enough. I was either going to talk to my mom or end it all. I walked into the living room and said, "Mom, I really need to talk to you." "Yes, what is it?" she said, without looking up from her paper. "Mom, I really need to talk to you," I said. Angrily she slammed the paper down into her lap and screamed, "Well, talk!" My throat felt like someone was strangling me. I couldn't breathe. All I could say was, "I love you, Mom," and I burst into tears. There was a long silence. I looked up at her and she was crying. We hugged and talked for over three hours!
I just wanted to write to tell you that my mom loves me. I didn't think that anyone cared for me at all. I can't believe that I was ready to kill myself. Thank God I talked to my mom.

Sincerely, Chelsea

❖ Having a good relationship with your family is critical to your life. God cares. Ask him to give you some clear direction and guidance during the next 10 days as you look into his plan for getting along with your family.

____ **proverbs 6:20-23** Parental protection

____ **proverbs 11:29; 15:27** Avoiding trouble

____ **Luke 2:41-52** Jesus and his parents

____ **ephesians 6:1-3** The children's role

____ **ephesians 6:4** The father's role

____ **colossians 3:18-21** It's everybody's job

____ **1 Thessalonians 5:11-15** Encouraging your family

____ **1 Timothy 5:8-10** Accepting responsibility

____ **Hebrews 12:5-11** The need for discipline

____ **1 peter 2:17** Showing respect

Today's Scripture: Proverbs 6:20-23

The main thing I remember or learned from this Scripture is . . .

_____
_____
_____
_____
_____

Here is what God is trying to teach me through this Scripture . . .

_____
_____
_____
_____
_____
_____

As a result of this, today I will . . .

_____
_____
_____
_____
_____

Right now I need to pray about . . .

_____
_____
_____
_____
_____

appointments with god

Today's Scripture: Proverbs 11:29; 15:27

The main thing I remember or learned from this Scripture is . . .

_____

_____

_____

_____

_____

Here is what God is trying to teach me through this Scripture . . .

_____

_____

_____

_____

_____

_____

As a result of this, today I will . . .

_____

_____

_____

_____

_____

Right now I need to pray about . . .

_____

_____

_____

_____

_____

Today's Scripture: Luke 2:41-52

The main thing I remember or learned from this Scripture is . . .

_____

_____

_____

_____

_____

Here is what God is trying to teach me through this Scripture . . .

_____

_____

_____

_____

_____

As a result of this, today I will . . .

_____

_____

_____

_____

_____

Right now I need to pray about . . .

_____

_____

_____

_____

_____

appointments with god

Today's Scripture: Ephesians 6:1-3

The main thing I remember or learned from this Scripture is . . .

_____

_____

_____

_____

_____

Here is what God is trying to teach me through this Scripture . . .

_____

_____

_____

_____

_____

_____

As a result of this, today I will . . .

_____

_____

_____

_____

_____

_____

Right now I need to pray about . . .

_____

_____

_____

_____

_____

Today's Scripture: Ephesians 6:4

The main thing I remember or learned from this Scripture is . . .

_____
_____
_____
_____
_____

Here is what God is trying to teach me through this Scripture . . .

_____
_____
_____
_____
_____
_____

As a result of this, today I will . . .

_____
_____
_____
_____
_____

Right now I need to pray about . . .

_____
_____
_____
_____
_____

appointments with god

Today's Scripture: Colossians 3:18-21

The main thing I remember or learned from this Scripture is . . .

_____

_____

_____

_____

_____

Here is what God is trying to teach me through this Scripture . . .

_____

_____

_____

_____

_____

As a result of this, today I will . . .

_____

_____

_____

_____

_____

Right now I need to pray about . . .

_____

_____

_____

_____

_____

DATE: _____   TIME: _____ AM PM

Today's Scripture: 1 Thessalonians 5:11-15
_____

The main thing I remember or learned from this Scripture is . . .
_____
_____
_____
_____
_____
_____
_____

Here is what God is trying to teach me through this Scripture . . .
_____
_____
_____
_____
_____
_____
_____

As a result of this, today I will . . .
_____
_____
_____
_____
_____
_____
_____

Right now I need to pray about . . .
_____
_____
_____
_____
_____
_____
_____

Today's Scripture: 1 Timothy 5:8-10

The main thing I remember or learned from this Scripture is . . .

_____

_____

_____

_____

_____

Here is what God is trying to teach me through this Scripture . . .

_____

_____

_____

_____

_____

_____

As a result of this, today I will . . .

_____

_____

_____

_____

_____

_____

Right now I need to pray about . . .

_____

_____

_____

_____

_____

_____

Today's Scripture: Hebrews 12:5-11
_____

The main thing I remember or learned from this Scripture is . . .
_____
_____
_____
_____
_____
_____

Here is what God is trying to teach me through this Scripture . . .
_____
_____
_____
_____
_____
_____
_____

As a result of this, today I will . . .
_____
_____
_____
_____
_____
_____

Right now I need to pray about . . .
_____
_____
_____
_____
_____
_____

appointments with god

Today's Scripture: 1 Peter 2:17

The main thing I remember or learned from this Scripture is . . .

_____
_____
_____
_____
_____
_____

Here is what God is trying to teach me through this Scripture . . .

_____
_____
_____
_____
_____
_____

As a result of this, today I will . . .

_____
_____
_____
_____
_____
_____

Right now I need to pray about . . .

_____
_____
_____
_____
_____
_____

Last year an amazing story appeared in the news. Twenty-two-year-old Graham Johnston worked nights at a local hotel to help pay for college. He drove the van that took hotel guests to and from the airport.

❧ One Saturday around 4:30 in the morning, as he was talking to some guests in the hotel lobby, he heard a woman scream just outside the main door. As he rushed outside, he could hear her cries for help, "He's going to kill me! He's going to kill me!" He ran up to a parked car and saw a man trying to drag a woman into his car. Without thinking, Johnston pounced on the man and broke them apart, giving the woman a chance to escape. The attacker, surprised that anyone would interfere, jumped into his car and sped off.

❧ Johnston used his cell phone to call for the police and medical help. The woman, Terry Peterson, had some bruises and cuts, but was not badly hurt. Ms. Peterson explained to police that she had met the man online and was out on a date with him. After several hours, she had begun to feel uncomfortable and told him that she wanted to end the date. He refused and she tried to escape. The man attacked her, and she screamed. That's when Graham Johnston got involved.

❧ A reporter for a local newspaper asked Mr. Johnston how it felt to be a hero. He replied, "I've never done anything like this before. I don't consider myself a hero. She was in desperate need of help, and fortunately, I happened to be that person. I did what anyone else would have done." The newspaper article entitled, "Unlikely Hero Saves Young Woman's Life" hit the stands a few days later.

❧ If you love hearing stories of people who made a difference—just by getting involved—you'll love reading the next 10 encounters in the Word. These people are some of God's unlikely heroes.

appointments with god

Today's Scripture: Exodus 2:1-10

The main thing I remember or learned from this Scripture is . . .

_____

_____

_____

_____

_____

Here is what God is trying to teach me through this Scripture . . .

_____

_____

_____

_____

_____

_____

As a result of this, today I will . . .

_____

_____

_____

_____

_____

_____

Right now I need to pray about . . .

_____

_____

_____

_____

_____

Today's Scripture: Joshua 2:1-24

The main thing I remember or learned from this Scripture is . . .

_____

_____

_____

_____

_____

_____

Here is what God is trying to teach me through this Scripture . . .

_____

_____

_____

_____

_____

_____

As a result of this, today I will . . .

_____

_____

_____

_____

_____

_____

Right now I need to pray about . . .

_____

_____

_____

_____

_____

_____

appointments with god

Today's Scripture: 1 Samuel 16:1-13

The main thing I remember or learned from this Scripture is . . .

_____

_____

_____

_____

_____

Here is what God is trying to teach me through this Scripture . . .

_____

_____

_____

_____

_____

As a result of this, today I will . . .

_____

_____

_____

_____

_____

Right now I need to pray about . . .

_____

_____

_____

_____

_____

Today's Scripture: 2 Kings 5:1-14

The main thing I remember or learned from this Scripture is . . .

_____

_____

_____

_____

_____

Here is what God is trying to teach me through this Scripture . . .

_____

_____

_____

_____

_____

As a result of this, today I will . . .

_____

_____

_____

_____

_____

Right now I need to pray about . . .

_____

_____

_____

_____

_____

appointments with god

Today's Scripture: 2 Kings 22:1, 2, 11-13
_____

The main thing I remember or learned from this Scripture is . . .
_____
_____
_____
_____
_____
_____

Here is what God is trying to teach me through this Scripture . . .
_____
_____
_____
_____
_____
_____
_____

As a result of this, today I will . . .
_____
_____
_____
_____
_____
_____

Right now I need to pray about . . .
_____
_____
_____
_____
_____

MY WORLD ❀ ENCOUNTERS 121-130

Today's Scripture: Matthew 3:1-17

The main thing I remember or learned from this Scripture is . . .

_____

_____

_____

_____

_____

_____

Here is what God is trying to teach me through this Scripture . . .

_____

_____

_____

_____

_____

_____

_____

As a result of this, today I will . . .

_____

_____

_____

_____

_____

_____

Right now I need to pray about . . .

_____

_____

_____

_____

_____

_____

appointments with god

Today's Scripture: Luke 1:26-45

The main thing I remember or learned from this Scripture is . . .

_____

_____

_____

_____

_____

Here is what God is trying to teach me through this Scripture . . .

_____

_____

_____

_____

_____

As a result of this, today I will . . .

_____

_____

_____

_____

_____

Right now I need to pray about . . .

_____

_____

_____

_____

_____

Today's Scripture: Acts 9:1-22

The main thing I remember or learned from this Scripture is . . .

_____

_____

_____

_____

_____

_____

Here is what God is trying to teach me through this Scripture . . .

_____

_____

_____

_____

_____

_____

As a result of this, today I will . . .

_____

_____

_____

_____

_____

Right now I need to pray about . . .

_____

_____

_____

_____

_____

appointments with god

Today's Scripture: Acts 23:12-22

The main thing I remember or learned from this Scripture is . . .

_____

_____

_____

_____

_____

_____

Here is what God is trying to teach me through this Scripture . . .

_____

_____

_____

_____

_____

_____

_____

As a result of this, today I will . . .

_____

_____

_____

_____

_____

_____

Right now I need to pray about . . .

_____

_____

_____

_____

_____

_____

Today's Scripture: 1 Timothy 4:11-16

The main thing I remember or learned from this Scripture is . . .

_____

_____

_____

_____

_____

_____

Here is what God is trying to teach me through this Scripture . . .

_____

_____

_____

_____

_____

_____

As a result of this, today I will . . .

_____

_____

_____

_____

_____

_____

Right now I need to pray about . . .

_____

_____

_____

_____

_____

_____

appointments with god

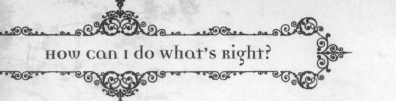

How can I do what's Right?

The first automobile I owned was an old 1970 Cutlass Supreme. It was a two-door coupe with a leather top, equipped with a 455 engine, a turbo 400 transmission, wide rear tires and a glass-pack exhaust. It was big, fast and loud. I loved that car. I drove it throughout my college days. When I decided to enter youth ministry, I thought I should buy a more sensible vehicle. So I parked the Cutlass at my parents' home and bought a little economy car.

❧ Last year my mom called to say that she was tired of having the Cutlass sit at her house. So I had it moved to mine. When I pulled the car off the trailer, it was a mess. It had been stored under a cover, but it was dirty. There were wasp nests all over it, and the engine wouldn't come close to starting. I decided I was going to restore the car.

❧ When I popped open the hood, I saw total chaos. The car had been through several "fixes" before I owned it and was in pretty bad shape. The wires and hoses looked like a plate of spaghetti. Parts were broken, dirty and some were just missing. I know a little bit about working on cars, but I had no idea where to begin. I just knew that I wanted to do it right.

❧ I got online and started researching 1970 Cutlass Supremes—then ordered an original owner's manual. It gave a detailed description of all the parts of the car and how they fit together to make the engine run. Following the directions in the manual, I was able to restore the engine back to its original condition. And it actually runs! Now I've got to work on the interior and get a new paint job on the outside.

❧ This series of appointments with God will provide some guidance for those situations that appear to be total chaos. You want to do what's right, but have no idea where to start. On your own, it's tough to sort out, but when you follow the strategy God provides in his Word (the original owner's manual!), you can repair the messy situation. During the next 10 days, you'll discover some essential guidelines for tackling these situations head-on.

Today's Scripture: Exodus 3:1-20

The main thing I remember or learned from this Scripture is . . .

_____

_____

_____

_____

_____

_____

Here is what God is trying to teach me through this Scripture . . .

_____

_____

_____

_____

_____

_____

As a result of this, today I will . . .

_____

_____

_____

_____

_____

Right now I need to pray about . . .

_____

_____

_____

_____

_____

_____

appointments with god

Today's Scripture: Numbers 27:12-23

The main thing I remember or learned from this Scripture is . . .

_____

_____

_____

_____

_____

Here is what God is trying to teach me through this Scripture . . .

_____

_____

_____

_____

_____

As a result of this, today I will . . .

_____

_____

_____

_____

_____

Right now I need to pray about . . .

_____

_____

_____

_____

_____

MY WORLD ✦ ENCOUNTERS 131-140

Today's Scripture: Judges 4:4-16

The main thing I remember or learned from this Scripture is . . .

_____

_____

_____

_____

_____

Here is what God is trying to teach me through this Scripture . . .

_____

_____

_____

_____

_____

As a result of this, today I will . . .

_____

_____

_____

_____

_____

Right now I need to pray about . . .

_____

_____

_____

_____

_____

appointments with god

Today's Scripture: Judges 7:1-25

The main thing I remember or learned from this Scripture is . . .

_____
_____
_____
_____
_____

Here is what God is trying to teach me through this Scripture . . .

_____
_____
_____
_____
_____
_____

As a result of this, today I will . . .

_____
_____
_____
_____
_____

Right now I need to pray about . . .

_____
_____
_____
_____
_____

Today's Scripture: 2 Samuel 5:1-10 _____

The main thing I remember or learned from this Scripture is . . . _____

_____

_____

_____

_____

_____

Here is what God is trying to teach me through this Scripture . . . _____

_____

_____

_____

_____

_____

As a result of this, today I will . . . _____

_____

_____

_____

_____

_____

Right now I need to pray about . . . _____

_____

_____

_____

_____

_____

_____

appointments with god

Today's Scripture: 1 Kings 2:1-4

The main thing I remember or learned from this Scripture is . . .

_____

_____

_____

_____

_____

_____

Here is what God is trying to teach me through this Scripture . . .

_____

_____

_____

_____

_____

_____

As a result of this, today I will . . .

_____

_____

_____

_____

_____

_____

Right now I need to pray about . . .

_____

_____

_____

_____

_____

DATE: _____ TIME: _____ AM PM

Today's Scripture: Jeremiah 23:1-4
_____

The main thing I remember or learned from this Scripture is . . .
_____
_____
_____
_____
_____

Here is what God is trying to teach me through this Scripture . . .
_____
_____
_____
_____
_____
_____
_____

As a result of this, today I will . . .
_____
_____
_____
_____
_____
_____

Right now I need to pray about . . .
_____
_____
_____
_____
_____

appointments with god

Today's Scripture: Jeremiah 38:1-13

The main thing I remember or learned from this Scripture is . . .

_____

_____

_____

_____

Here is what God is trying to teach me through this Scripture . . .

_____

_____

_____

_____

_____

As a result of this, today I will . . .

_____

_____

_____

_____

_____

Right now I need to pray about . . .

_____

_____

_____

_____

Today's Scripture: Daniel 1:3-21

The main thing I remember or learned from this Scripture is . . .

_____

_____

_____

_____

Here is what God is trying to teach me through this Scripture . . .

_____

_____

_____

_____

_____

As a result of this, today I will . . .

_____

_____

_____

_____

Right now I need to pray about . . .

_____

_____

_____

_____

appointments with god

Today's Scripture: Hebrews 11:24-40

The main thing I remember or learned from this Scripture is . . .

_____

_____

_____

_____

_____

Here is what God is trying to teach me through this Scripture . . .

_____

_____

_____

_____

_____

_____

As a result of this, today I will . . .

_____

_____

_____

_____

_____

Right now I need to pray about . . .

_____

_____

_____

_____

_____

_____

HOW CAN I SPEAK UP FOR THOSE WHO CAN'T?

Once upon a time a poor, blind, old widow lived in a run-down trailer park. A land developer intended to build a strip mall on that property—and get rich. Over several months' time, all of the woman's neighbors took the developer's generous offer and moved—but the widow refused again and again. This trailer was all she had left of the life she'd shared with her late husband.

❧ One day the developer had a devious plan. Because the widow was blind, he disguised his voice and approached her. Pretending to be from the government, he did a "routine inspection of her property for tax purposes." After looking around for a few minutes, he had her sign some papers to "verify that she owned the property." In reality, the papers signed the property over to him. He left with the prospect of building the mall and becoming wealthy.

❧ Soon, the bulldozers arrived and started knocking down all the trailers. When they came to the widow's door and told her she would have to leave, she didn't understand. "This can't be," she pleaded. "This is my home! My husband and I bought it together!" Because she had signed the papers, there was nothing to be done.

❧ The next day the local newspaper carried the story with a picture of the poor, blind, old widow sitting at the curb in a lawn chair while the bulldozer leveled her home. A lawyer read the story and decided to do something. He met with the woman and represented her free of charge. They took the developer to court and won! Not only was the developer convicted of fraud and thrown into jail, but his company had to build the woman a big, brand-new house right on the site where her trailer once sat.

❧ In a follow-up newspaper story, the widow expressed amazement that someone cared enough to help a lady who couldn't help herself. Surely God smiles when stories like this one take place. Over the next 10 days, you'll encounter similar true stories from the Word.

____ joshua 20:1-9 A safe place

____ ruth 2:1-20 A poor widow's needs

____ 1 kings 21:1-26 A murderer confronted

____ nehemiah 5:1-13 Defending the poor

____ esther 7:1-10 A nation saved

____ jeremiah 34:8-22 Freedom for slaves

____ mark 9:36, 37, 42 Caring for children

____ luke 16:19-31 Eternal comfort

____ philemon 8-18 A changed friend

____ james 2:1-10 Favoritism forbidden

Today's Scripture: Joshua 20:1-9

The main thing I remember or learned from this Scripture is . . .

_____

_____

_____

_____

_____

Here is what God is trying to teach me through this Scripture . . .

_____

_____

_____

_____

_____

As a result of this, today I will . . .

_____

_____

_____

_____

_____

Right now I need to pray about . . .

_____

_____

_____

_____

_____

Today's Scripture: Ruth 2:1-20

The main thing I remember or learned from this Scripture is . . .

_____

_____

_____

_____

_____

Here is what God is trying to teach me through this Scripture . . .

_____

_____

_____

_____

_____

As a result of this, today I will . . .

_____

_____

_____

_____

Right now I need to pray about . . .

_____

_____

_____

_____

_____

appointments with god

Today's Scripture: 1 Kings 21:1-26
_____

The main thing I remember or learned from this Scripture is . . .
_____
_____
_____
_____
_____
_____

Here is what God is trying to teach me through this Scripture . . .
_____
_____
_____
_____
_____
_____

As a result of this, today I will . . .
_____
_____
_____
_____
_____
_____

Right now I need to pray about . . .
_____
_____
_____
_____
_____

Today's Scripture: Nehemiah 5:1-13

The main thing I remember or learned from this Scripture is . . .

_____

_____

_____

_____

Here is what God is trying to teach me through this Scripture . . .

_____

_____

_____

_____

_____

As a result of this, today I will . . .

_____

_____

_____

_____

_____

Right now I need to pray about . . .

_____

_____

_____

_____

_____

appointments with god

Today's Scripture: Esther 7:1-10
_____

The main thing I remember or learned from this Scripture is . . .
_____
_____
_____

Here is what God is trying to teach me through this Scripture . . .
_____
_____
_____
_____
_____

As a result of this, today I will . . .
_____
_____
_____
_____

Right now I need to pray about . . .
_____
_____
_____
_____

Today's Scripture: Jeremiah 34:8-22

The main thing I remember or learned from this Scripture is . . .

Here is what God is trying to teach me through this Scripture . . .

As a result of this, today I will . . .

Right now I need to pray about . . .

appointments with god

Today's Scripture: Mark 9:36, 37, 42

The main thing I remember or learned from this Scripture is . . .

_____

_____

_____

_____

_____

Here is what God is trying to teach me through this Scripture . . .

_____

_____

_____

_____

_____

_____

As a result of this, today I will . . .

_____

_____

_____

_____

_____

_____

Right now I need to pray about . . .

_____

_____

_____

_____

_____

_____

DATE: _____   TIME: _____   AM   PM

Today's Scripture: Luke 16:19-31
_____

The main thing I remember or learned from this Scripture is . . .
_____
_____
_____
_____
_____
_____

Here is what God is trying to teach me through this Scripture . . .
_____
_____
_____
_____
_____
_____

As a result of this, today I will . . .
_____
_____
_____
_____
_____
_____

Right now I need to pray about . . .
_____
_____
_____
_____
_____
_____

Today's Scripture: Philemon 8-18

The main thing I remember or learned from this Scripture is . . .

Here is what God is trying to teach me through this Scripture . . .

As a result of this, today I will . . .

Right now I need to pray about . . .

Today's Scripture: James 2:1-10

The main thing I remember or learned from this Scripture is . . .

_____

_____

_____

_____

_____

Here is what God is trying to teach me through this Scripture . . .

_____

_____

_____

_____

_____

As a result of this, today I will . . .

_____

_____

_____

_____

Right now I need to pray about . . .

_____

_____

_____

_____

_____

appointments with god

scripture index

appointments with god

also from standard publishing...

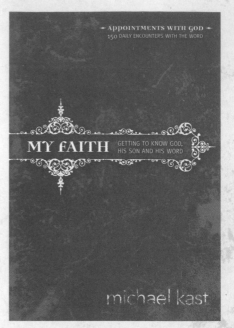

You've worked your way through 150 appointments with God. Now what? Check out *My Faith: Getting to Know God, His Son and His Word.* You'll find 150 more daily encounters. Included inside you'll find these sections:

❧ *Getting to Know God*: Who is God? Who is the Holy Spirit? Discover the character and promises of God.

❧ *Getting to Know Jesus*: Take a deep look at the miracles and parables of Jesus, his life experiences, his teachings and his last week.

❧ *Getting to Know His Word*: Why study the Bible? What are some important Old Testament and New Testament Scriptures? Take a look at some people in the Bible who followed God—and some who did not.